Be Proud Of Me

a play by Stan's Cafe

ISBN 978-1-913185-17-6

Published by Stan's Cafe
Birmingham, UK
2020

www.stanscafe.co.uk

Be Proud Of Me © Stan's Cafe 2003
Production photos © Ed Dimsdale 2004
Slide photos © Ed Dimsdale & Stan's Cafe 2003
Publication © Stan's Cafe 2020

Contents:

Be Proud Of Me 1
Bonus Material
Original programme notes 66

Be Proud Of Me

[1 Window]

C: My name is Dawson, my name is Rogers. I, I come from England.
I, my name is Mountford, I come from England.
I am a, I'm here on business. I'm a salesman. I'm a dentist. I'm a salesman.
I am thirty four years old. I live in England. I travel.
It is a long way. I am on my own. I speak little german.
My name is Michael. My name is John.
I have never been here before.

[2 Sky]

I like it here. The weather is fine. I live in England in a small house. There are two bedrooms. There's a fireplace in the dining room and a table with fruit on it. There is a bathroom. I'm on my own. There is no garden. I have been travelling for a week, a month, a year. I'm ill.
I've never been here before. This is my first visit.

[3 Eye]

I've been to the park. Everyone is very friendly. I like dancing. I run. I like swimming. I am booked into a hotel. It is the autumn. I have everything I need. I have a beautiful room in a hotel, with a view of the cathedral. I have a girlfriend, she is ill. Is it always this hot?

[4 Strip light]

Is the weather always this hot? I'm ill. I'm on my own. I like walks in the countryside. I like drinking in bars.
Is there a church near here? Can you tell me what I should see? Can you tell me what I should do?

[5 Scuzzy room]
   I need to tell you something. I'm staying in the Hotel Excelsior. My flight leaves in the morning. Is it safe here? There's been an accident. I need to speak to you. I need to report something. Something has happened. I need to see you.
A: *[Enter]*

[6 Childhood dining room]

C: I have something to declare.
A: Ich habe etwas zu verzollen.
C: I am here on business.
A: Ich bin auf einer geschaeftsreise hier. Ask me something else.
C: Woher kommen sie?
A: Ich bin aus England.
C: Good... alright... wie heissen sie?
A: Ich heisse Susan. Wie heissen sie?
C: Ich heisse Michael.
A: Haben sie ein schwester?
C: Ja ... Sie heisst Susan. Ich bin auf sie stoltz.
A: You're better at this than me.
C: Shall I come with you?
A: No, I've got to go alone. My flight leaves at midnight.
C: Can I call you?
A: I don't have a telephone.
C: When will you come home?
A: I don't know. It's a one-way ticket. Will you miss me?
C: I might. I bought you this *[hands her the necklace]* for luck.
A: It's beautiful. Do you think I'll need it?
C: No, you'll be alright.
A: Thank you. What will you do if I don't come back?
C: I'll look for you.

[7 Alpine cafe reflection]

C: My flight was delayed.
I was delayed at the airport.
I was held up at immigration.
I will carry that myself.
[Gets photo of Claire out of his pocket]

[8 Alpine cafe]

He was moving too fast.
I did not see the sign.
He ran into the back of my car.

[9 Alpine café table]

I could not stop in time.
He did not stop. He did not give way.
She is a chemist. I was.

[10 Scuzzy room curtain]

C: I know, I understand.
A: Stand up Michael, they're calling your flight.

[11 Wasteland]

C: *[Looks up to sky and follows airplane flying overhead]*

[12 Airplane]
[13 Airplane overhead]
[14 Airplane]
[15 Airplane disappearing in distance]
[16 Escalator 1]
[17 Escalator 2]
[18 Railway ceiling]
[19 Railway ceiling 2]

C: *[Turning]*
A: *[Enters]*

[20 Airport Corridor 2]

A: *[As passport control]* Pass bitte. Pass. Passport.
C: Sorry. *[Hands over passport]*
A: Where are you travelling to?
C: Frankfurt.
A: What is the purpose of your visit?
C: Work, I'm here on business.
A: How long will you be staying?
C: Five days.
A: Can I see your wallet?
C: *[Hands over wallet]*
A: Where are you staying?
C: The Hotel Continental. What are you looking for?
A: *[Finds photo in wallet]* Ist das ihre Freundin?
C: Yes, I'm meeting her in Germany.
A: *[Puts photo back and returns wallet then passport]* Enjoy your trip... Mr. Mountford.
C: *[Looks at his photo in the passport]*

[21 Pier slide]

C: I never thought I'd find myself here.
I mean, this situation, being here with you.
I brought you this *[Passport falls out of his pocket]*
A: *[Bends slowly and picks it up]* I think this is yours, you dropped it.
C: Thank you. Excuse me. Entschuldigung Sie bitte.

[22 Airport taxis]

C: Which gate for Frankfurt please?
A: Für Berlin es ist einundzwanzig.
C: I'm late for the Frankfurt flight.
A: Your train leaves from Platform 5.
C: Can't I fly direct?
A: You can take a bus from Milan.
C: How long does that take?

A: The ferry to Hamburg takes about two hours.
C: I change at Hamburg for Frankfurt?
A: Non, non, non, changez at Paris pour Bruxelles
C: And can I fly from there?
A: You take the express to Vienna for the connection to Zagreb.
C: Do I need to make a reservation?
A: For how many people?
C: I'm travelling alone.
A: To Prague?
C: No.
A: To Vilnius?
C: No.
A: To Belgrade?
C: No, to Frankfurt.
A: Fur Frankfurt es ist achtzehn. *[Exit]*
C: Danke.

[23 Railway station]
[24 Millennium Point close up]
[25 Millennium Point medium]
[26 Millennium Point long shot]

C: *[Moves upstage]*

[27 Tube train]
[28 Tube train]
[29 Tube train]

A: *[Enters with suitcase bumps into C]* Oh... sorry.
C: *[Grabs her arm]* Susan?

[30 Underground station]

A: No. Do I know you?
C: Sorry, I thought you were someone else... very sorry.
A: That's okay. *[Goes to leave]*
C: Actually, you might be able to help me... I'm lost... I'm looking for the Hotel Excelsior.

A: *[Puts down suitcase]* Ah yes. Come out of here.

[31 Subway]

C: *[Copies some of the directions]*
A: Walk straight ahead down the main street. At the post office turn right. Carry on over the bridge until you reach a large square.
Sie fahren bis dem Platz.

[32 Hercules sculpture]

Hotel Opera ist neben dem kino.
C: Opposite the Cathedral.
A: You turn right. Carry on over the bridge. Keep going till you reach the river.
C: I follow the road for Cafe Michelle.

[33 Street lights]

A: Le Cafe Michelle est en face du cinema, sur Place de la Reine. Tu prends le metro. Descendez a la station Universite. The Main campus is down by the river.

[34 Arcade sign]

A: Walk straight down the main street. At the post office turn right. It's only ten minutes walk...

C: ...walk or is it possible to get a bus?
A: ...the bus from Kapelstrasse.

[35 St. Petersburg mist]

A: Get off at the estate when you see three tower blocks to your right. The largest has twenty four apartments. Press the buzzer for number eighteen. When they let you in don't take the elevator, take the stairs. He won't be there until eleven. His secretary will let you in. Don't be late. He

won't wait for you.
C: Is he expecting me?
A: I'd better go. *[Exit]*
C: Will he know who I am? *[Looks around and spots suitcase. He slowly goes to pick it up. As he lifts it the slide changes]*

[36 Rooftop]

C: Hello? Hello? I'm here. I have a delivery.
Can you hear me? I made it. I'm on time.
I've done what you wanted.

[37 Roof lens flare]

C: It's finished.
I want it wrapped up.
Where are you?
I want to go home. *[Spots necklace on ground]*

[38 Close up of necklace]

C: *[Bends down and picks up necklace]*

[39 Wall door pipe]

C: This isn't what I want.
Can we stop here?
I have what you want. Do you want to see?
I'll show you. *[Moves DS and holds case open above his head, nothing falls out]*

[40 Hotel Lobby]

A: *[Enters with chair looking at C standing with open suitcase. She puts chair down USR. As hotel receptionist]* Is everything alright?
C: *[Looks around and closes case]*
A: Can I get you anything?

C: Um...
A: Would you like me to put that in the hotel safe?
C: No *[Closes clasps on case]* thank you. I'd like to make a reservation please.
A: For dinner?
C: No, I'd like to book a room.
A: You'd like to book another room?
C: No, I'd like a room for myself for four nights.
A: You'd like to extend your stay?
C: No, you don't understand, I'd like a room for tonight and three other nights.
A: But you're booked into Room 201 tonight Mr Mountford.
C: 201?
A: Oh... here's your passport *[Hands him passport]*
C: Could I have my key please?
A: You picked it up this morning.
C: Yes, of course. *[Feels in pockets]*
A: Is everything alright?
C: *[Finds key]*
A: Would you like something sent up to your room?
  Would you like dinner in your room?
C: Um... No, thank you.
A: Is everything alright with the room? *[Gestures to screen and slide changes to hotel room]*

[41 Hotel room kettle]

C: Yes thank you it's... *[Sits in the chair and puts down case]*
A: Is it too cold? Is it too warm? Would you like more blankets? Would you like anything?
C: No thank you, I have everything I need.
A: Would you like me to open a window ?
  I'm afraid they're locked.
  Would you like a shower?
  I'm sorry the towels are dirty.
C: *[Picks up case, gets files out and looks through them]*

[42 Scuzzy room]

A: Would you like something from the bar?
I'm afraid it's closed.
Would you like to change your room?
I'm afraid we're fully booked at the moment.
Would you like room service?
I'm sorry the kitchen is shut.
Shall I arrange an alarm call for you?
I'm afraid there's no-one on duty at that time.
Would you like to take a bath?
I'm afraid there's no hot water.

[43 Hotel room kettle]

C: *[Closes case and hands A the files]*
Could you put these in the hotel safe please?
A: Of course.
C: *[Looks at floor and slide changes to Claire's flat]*

[44 Claire's flat window]

A: *[As Claire]* You should go to bed.
C: Yeah... I... I'll just go back to the hotel I think... I'm feeling pretty rough.
A: No, no, no... you can stay here.
C: No... it's fine, I'll go back... it's okay...
A: No, I'd like it if you stayed. I mean you can make yourself at home can't you? You can have a bath... have something to eat... watch TV... relax, whatever you want to do.
C: Well, if you don't mind.
A: Course I don't mind.
C: Do you have to go to work?
A: Yes.
C: No-one's indispensable are they?
A: I am.
C: Well, I'm sure you are... it's just I'm ill... I need your medical expertise.
A: I keep telling you I'm a chemist.
C: Same thing.

A: It is not the same. I've got to go sorry. I've got to drop these off today.
C: Okay.
A: I'd love to stay and nurse your germs but I can't. Actually what I can do though is leave you my keys. *[Produces keys]* Now, I don't do this for everyone you know!
C: I should hope not.
A: Pay attention.
C: Right.
A: *[Showing the keys]* This is for the main door downstairs, this is the Chubb lock for this flat and this is the Yale. Got that?
C: Yes... I think so. Any house rules?
A: Yes, don't touch anything, sit in that chair and don't move.
C: Okay.
A: Apart from that just relax.
C: Sounds perfect.
A: Good, there you go. *[Hands over keys]*
C: Thanks.
A: I'll be back about six.
C: If you worked a bit harder and faster you could get home sooner .
A: What are you saying?
C: Well you know... to look after me.
A: You're so cheeky.
C: I'm ill!
A: I know but I've got to work. If you're better when I get back at six we can go for a meal. Alright?
C: Alright, good incentive to get better.
   [They kiss]
A: I'll see you later. *[Goes to exit]*
C: You've got it now!
A: Ah... *[Exit]*
C: *[Pockets keys. Scans the room. Moves DSR]*

[45 Office Wall]

A: *[Enters as secretary]* Kann ich ihnen helfen?

C: *[Looks round]*
A: Can I help you?
C: Ah yes, I have an appointment with a Mr Nowicki.
A: I'm afraid there's no-one here by that name.
C: No, there is, he's expecting me, I have an appointment, 11 o'clock.
A: What's your name?
C: Dawson.
A: I'm sorry Mr Dawson, there's no one here by the name of Nowicki.
C: No, he's expecting me. I was told to come here. He has something for me. It's very important.
A: What's your name?
C: Mountford.
A: I'm sorry Mr. Mountford you've made a mistake, there's no one here called Nowicki.
C: No, this is the place. I have an appointment, eleven o'clock, it's very important, he should be here. Look could I make a telephone call?
A: What's your name?
C: Is he in?
A: What's your name?
C: Rogers.
A: Why don't you sit down Mr. Rogers. I'll tell Mr. Nowicki you're here.
C: Thank you. *[Turns away and sees blood on the grass]*

[46 Blood on grass]

A: Is anything wrong Mr. Rogers?
C: *[Turns back]*

[47 Wall]

C: No... everything's fine, thank you.
A: *[Exits]*
C: *[Takes a pill. Sits]*

[48 Warehouse]

C: [Folds arms and looks SR]

[49 Wakefield station]

C: [Looks at watch]

[50 Barca airport]

C: [Leans forward]

[51 Empty airport]

C: [Opens case]

[52 Transit bus]

C: [Puts case down]

[53 Barca door]

C: [Gets wallet out. Takes photo out. Puts wallet back]

[54 Millennium Point cafe]

C: [Leans forward with photo]

[55 Main cafe]

A: [Enters as waitress with table] Kann ich ihnen helfen?
C: Um...
A: Wass mochten sie?
C: Um...
A: Café / bier?
C: Bier bitte.
A: Kleine?
C: Grosse please, danke.
A: [Exits then re-enters with chair and mug and sits at table]

[56 City Street]

A: *[As tourist]* Do you mind if I sit here?
C: Fine.
A: Do you mind if I smoke? Would you like a cigarette?
C: Do you have one?
A: I don't smoke! What a lovely day. What terrible weather we're having. Are you here on holiday?
C: No... I'm a...
A: I'm on holiday.
C: Right....
A: I'm lost. Can you help me?
C: Actually, I'm just visiting myself...
A: Are you married?
C: Well...
A: I'm single, separated, divorced. I'm a widow.
C: Sorry to hear that.
A: Can I kiss you?
C: Um... I don't...
A: I know a very good night club very near here.
C: Right. Look do you come here often?
A: Would you like to go somewhere else?
C: Do you drink in this bar regularly?
A: Would you like to go back to my house?
C: You might be able to help me.
A: Are you free later this evening?
C: I'm looking for this woman.
   [Shows A a photograph, she takes it]

[57 Heineken Sign]

A: *[As English woman]* Is she English?
C: Yes, we're old school friends, we lost touch, I've been trying to find her. I think she lives round here somewhere.
A: Sorry.
C: No?
A: No. *[Hands photo back]*
C: Thanks. *[Looks down at photo]*

[58 Ikon Cafe]

C: She may be something to do with the university I think.
A: *[As an Italian]* Ah si, si.
C: Her parents are worried about her. I'm trying to be discreet.
A: Studente?
C: A lecturer I think.
A: Professore. *[Takes photo]*
C: Si. Do you recognise her?
A: No lo so no, no.
C: You're sure?
A: Si. Certo.
C: She works in the science department.
A: Ah, studiato musica.
C: You study music?
A: Me dispiace.
C: That's okay.
A: Cafe?
C: No.
A: Scusi... scusi... cafe, due cafe... ah.

[59 Blurry Cafe]

C: *[Looking at photo]* C'est tres important... excuse moi, ma francais est un peu mal... c'est tres important que je trouve la femme ici. *[Shows A photo]*
A: *[As French]* Ah oui. *[She looks]* Ah!
C: Tu reconnais?
A: A t'elle le cheveux court?
C: Ah oui peut etre... it's an old photograph.
A: Ah oui!
C: It's very important I find her. I have some good news for her.... des nouvelles bonnes?
A: Pardon?
C: You've seen her?
A: Ah oui, elle etait la hier soir.
C: Sorry?
A: La hier soir.

C: She was in here yesterday?
A: Oui.
C: You saw her?
A: Oui.
C: Have you seen her before?
A: Oui.
C: Could she be in this evening?
A: Oui peut etre, c'est possible.... je ne sais.
C: Merci beaucoup!
A: Bonne chance.
C: Merci. *[Stares at photo]*

[60 Eyes]

A: *[As Claire, looking at C]* Ist das ihre freunden?
C: *[Looking at Claire]* Sorry?

[61 Main Cafe]

A: Is that your girlfriend?
C: *[Putting away photo]* No, no she's, she's a friend. You're English?
A: Yes.
C: So am I.
A: Really?
C: You might have guessed.
A: Yes, I did notice.
C: I thought I was blending in!
A: Are you waiting for someone?
C: No, no I was on my way back to my hotel. I saw this bar and thought it looked nice, so called in.
A: Are you on holiday?
C: No... I'm here for work... just a few days.
A: Oh right.
C: You?
A: No, I live here.
C: Wow.
A: Five, no six years now.
C: It's a beautiful city, you're very lucky!

A: It is... I like it very much.
C: So you work here?
A: Yes I do.
C: What do you do?
A: I'm a chemist.
C: A pharmacy... chemist shop?
A: No... not quite plasters and painkillers, more test tubes and bunsen burners.
C: Right, sorry.
A: I'm sort of part of the university.
C: Sounds very interesting.
A: Not really... so what about you?
C: I'm a... I'm...
A: *[As Boss]* What do you do?

[62 Briefing room]

C: I... *[Stands up]* Look, she won't ask will she?
A: Of course she'll ask you, what are you going to say?
C: If she asks I'll think of something.
A: That's not good enough, you need to know before you go.
C: Alright, I... I work in antiques... I deliver expensive antiques by hand across Europe.
A: Antiques? What are you talking about? What do you know about antiques?
C: What does she know about antiques?
A: I don't know, she might be an expert for all you know. Think of something simple. Something you can lie about easily.
C: Alright... alright... *[Sits]*
A: So if she asks you what you do? What do you say?
C: I'm a...

[63 Cafe]

C: This is really boring... I'm a salesman.
A: *[As Claire]* Right.
C: I sell office equipment, there I've bored myself telling you that.

29

A: No, no, somebody's got to do it.
C: And it might as well be me.
A: We all need stationery. I've got a lot of it myself.
C: I may have supplied it.
A: Well, thank you very much.
C: A pleasure!
A: So have you had chance to see the city at all?
C: Not really no, it's very bad actually, I've just been from my hotel to this bar pretty much. I got really lost earlier. I haven't got a guide book yet. I've just got one of those maps from McDonalds and I don't think they're very accurate are they?
A: No, I don't think so!
C: I have been to two McDonalds though.
A: Oh right so you've been out then!
C: Yeah I've not been wasting my time.
A: Where are you staying?
C: The Hotel Excelsior.

[64 Briefing room]

A: *[As Boss]* No you're not!
C: The Belle Vue.
A: That's in Paris. Look we briefed you on this.
C: It's a lot to remember, I'm tired… the… the Hotel Opera.
A: Which is where?
C: The Old Town.
A: Which they call the Gothic Quarter.
C: Right.

[65 Cafe]

C: I'm at the Hotel Opera.
A: Very nice.
C: It is, I've got a view of the cathedral from my window.
A: Lovely.
C: Right in the heart of the Gothic Quarter.
A: Very good.
C: It's very classy.

A: Very classy.
C: So where do you live?
A: I live in the west part of the city, it's not quite so classy, bit studenty, a bit rundown but I like it, lots of good bars.
C: Sorry, do you want a drink?
A: No, no, I'm fine.
C: Sure?
A: Yes, I have to get back to work.
C: Right. Look I shouldn't really ask this but…
A: Ah?
C: No it's OK, don't worry.
A: Right.
C: You don't happen to have an hour or two free over the next couple of days?
A: Ah, I can't.
C: It's just it would be great to have someone who knows the city, knows more than just McDonalds, to show me the sights.
A: I'd love to say yes, but I can't.
C: Just an hour or two?
A: I'm sorry, we're working on a very big project and it's coming to an end in a day or two, so I'm really busy.
C: That's fine.
A: Sorry.
C: That's alright, I understand. *[Leans back in chair]*

[66 Briefing Room]

A: *[As Boss]* No, it is not fine! You've got two, maybe three days before this project ends. You have to get inside her flat. You have to make her meet you.
C: I know all this, we've been through all this!
A: So what are you going to do?
C: Don't worry about it.
A: I am worried.
C: You can trust me. I've been waiting for this for years. I know what I'm doing.
A: So you have a strategy?
C: Yes.

A: You know what you're going to say?
C: Yes, when I'm there I'll persuade her.
A: That's not good enough.
C: I'll make her see me.
A: Don't mess this up!
C: I won't. I won't let her go.
A: Okay.

[67 Cafe]

A: *[As Claire]* Okay, you win I'll give you one hour.
C: I'll buy you dinner.
A: Alright two hours.
C: You're very easily persuaded.
A: Yes, I am aren't I!
C: No arm twisting or anything. Look I really appreciate that, thank you.
A: I don't even know your name.
C: No sorry. *[Stands]*
A: Does that make me look cheap?
C: Well a bit.
A: You don't mind though?
C: No, it's John.
A: Nice to meet you John, I'm Claire.
C: Claire. Nice to meet you Claire.
A: Look, I've really got to go.
C: Of course.
A: Is 7.30 alright tomorrow?
C: Whatever's best for you.
A: Yep, that's good.
C: Where shall we meet? Actually we'd better meet here!
A: Yes.
C: I can find here or a McDonalds!
A: Let's make it here.
C: Yeah, probably nicer.
A: Alright I'll see you tomorrow.
C: Yeah. I'll look forward to it. *[Follows A to edge of stage]*
A: See you then.
C: Yeah, see you and don't work too hard!

A: Oh I will.
C: Bye.
A: See you. *[Exit]*
C: *[Looks back into room]*

[68 Whole mug]

C: *[Sits and picks up mug]*

[69 Broken mug]

C: *[Puts mug down]*

[70 Whole mug]

C: *[Looks up]*

[71 Fluorescent tube]
[72 Sky]

C: *[Lowers head]*

[73 Shooting Landscape]

C: *[Leans forward, focusing on ground]*

[74 Blood on grass]

C: *[Looking at his feet]*

[75 Feet]

C: *[Looking up, head in hands]*

[76 Cell]

C: I am ill.
I have high blood pressure.
I am allergic.

	I think it is infected.

       I'm ill.
- A: *[Enters with gun in case]*
- C: I have high blood pressure.
  I'm allergic.
  I think it's infected. *[Sitting on edge of table]*
- A: Did you take your temperature?
- C: I've a pain in my arm.
- A: Does it hurt?
- C: My wrist hurts.
- A: A lot or a little?
- C: I think I've sprained/broken my ankle.
- A: Your leg must be X-rayed.
  You must go to hospital.
  You must stay in bed for a few days.
- C: I fell down and hurt my back.
- A: Where does it hurt?
- C: My feet are swollen.
  I've burned / cut / bruised myself.
  I have an upset stomach.
  I have indigestion.
  My appetite's gone.
  I think I've got food poisoning.
  I can't eat / sleep. *[A forces C to look up]*

[77 Fluorescent tube]

- A: How long have you had the pain?
- C: I am a diabetic *[Looks down]*.

[78 Window]

- A: Open your mouth.
- C: I have a heart condition.
- A: Put out your tongue.
- C: My nose keeps bleeding.
- A: Please stand up. *[Listens to C's chest]*
- A: Breathe in.
- C: I have earache.

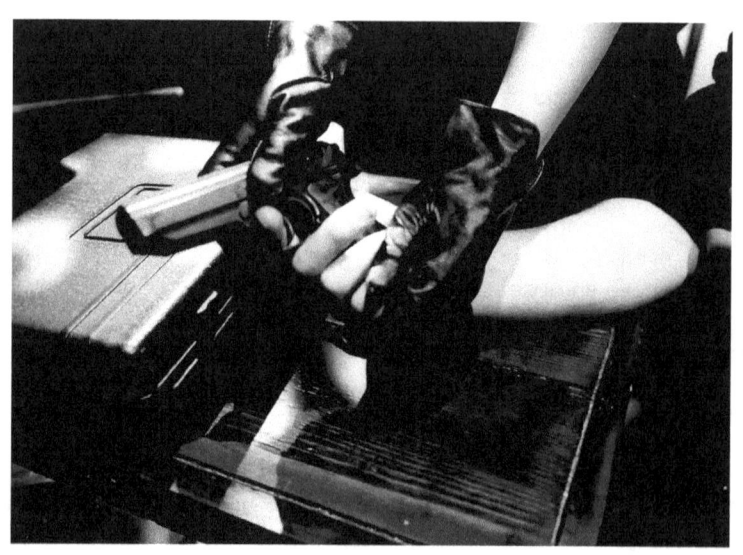

A: Hold your breath. *[Lets C go]*
I'll have to have a blood specimen.
What medicines are you taking?
C: I take this medicine, could you give me
another prescription?
A: *[Putting gloves on and magazine in gun]* I'll give you an antibiotic / a pain killer / a sedative.
Take these pills / this medicine.
Take this three times a day.
Take this to the chemist.
I'll give you an injection.
Roll up your sleeve.
C: *[Rolls sleeve, arm on table]* I have difficulty in breathing.
A: *[Putting gun in C's hand]* The nerve is exposed, the tooth must be extracted.
Come and see me in two days / a week's time.
C: I feel dizzy.
I feel sick/shivery.
I feel sick.
I keep vomiting.
I think I've caught 'flu.
I've got a heavy cold.
I've had the cold since yesterday.
I've had it for a few hours.
You're hurting me. *[Hands over an envelope of cash]*
When do you think I'll be able to go home?
A: You should not travel for at least five days.
Nothing to worry about.
Now if you'll excuse me I have another appointment.
[Closes case and puts it behind suitcase and sits]
C: *[Stands and scans room with gun]*

[79 Night window]

C: I feel better now.
Everything will be fine.
I have health insurance. *[Looks down at gun held by side]*

[80 Arm and gun]

C: *[Looks up]*

[81 Restaurant memory silhouette]
[82 Cafe long shot with Claire]

C: *[Puts gun into coat pocket]*

[83 Cafe painting]

C: *[Turns into the scene]*
A: *[Sitting at table as Claire]*
C: I'm sorry I'm late.
A: That's alright.
C: It wasn't my fault this time.
A: Really?
C: Something's happened I think. There's police everywhere.
A: Oh yes, there's a huge demonstration today, I should have told you.
C: I tried to come a back way but I've only got that McDonald's map.
A: That stupid map.
C: That's been a good map that!
A: It's been a rubbish map. I'm gonna buy you a guide book.
C: Anyway, thanks for waiting I thought you might have gone.
A: No, of course not.
C: So what do you want to do? Where shall we go? Do you want to eat here?
A: No.
C: No? Okay, well it's your city.
A: True, but it's your last couple of days.
C: That's also true. I'm rubbish at making decisions though.
A: Well looking at this scientifically I think we have a choice of two things. Either we do something that you've already done that you like,
C: That could be good.
A: Or we do something risky and new.
C: That could be better!

A: It could couldn't it!
C: Do you have something in mind?
A: Actually I do have a plan.
C: Does it involve drinking?
A: Yeah.
C: I thought it might.
A: No listen, you know where I live, where the flat is?
C: Yeah.
A: Can you remember... just a couple of streets away there's a market... *[As she talks she reaches into C's pocket, takes out the gun and puts it on the table. C looks around startled. A continues talking as if all is normal]*

[84 Claire smiling]

A: ...well just near to there, if you just go down a little side street, there's a really brilliant jazz bar...

[85 Claire pointing]

A: ...now I know you're funny about jazz but it's alright there's no jazz till later.
C: *[Puts the gun back in his pocket]*

[86 Bar beer pumps]

C: Did you say jazz?
A: It's fine. If you get there early it's great, a friend of mine's the barman and they do absolutely fantastic cocktails. *[She gets the gun out of C's pocket again. C looks around, picks up gun, A grabs C's hand and points it and the gun at her own head]*

[87 Claire smiling]

A: *[Talking normally]* The martinis are the best in the city, I guarantee it. So I reckon we go there first and when we've done that if we want we can go and eat.

[88 Claire staring]

C: There's been a mistake here. This isn't our table.
A: I don't mind really.
C: This isn't what I wanted.
A: Italian? It depends how hungry you are.
C: I want to go back.
A: Whatever, it's up to you.

[89 Claire gesturing]

C: I don't want this.
A: Alright, we'll go for one drink and then we'll find somewhere to eat.
C: It's making me ill... it's... I want to go home!
[Snatches gun away and puts it back in his pocket]

[90 Wine bottles]

A: John? Are you alright?
C: Sorry, yeah, I'm fine... I'm fine.

[91 Briefing room]

A: *[As Boss]* You don't look fine and I don't think you can handle this. I don't think you're going to deliver.
C: Of course I can handle it.
   I'm going whether you like it or not.
A: You're too involved, it's too personal.
C: Of course it's personal, that's why I'm going!

[92 Bottles]

A: *[As Claire]* You really don't look well.
C: No. Are you okay?
A: Yeah I'm fine, look perhaps we should go back to the flat.
C: Maybe we should. Sorry I've ruined the evening.
A: No that's fine.
C: I don't know what's the matter with me.
A: I'll cook.

C: I might not be able to eat it.
A: That's alright I'm an awful cook. Come on, let's go.
C: Yeah. *[They stand]*
A: *[Touching C's forehead]* You're hot, you're really hot!
C: Yeah.
A: Alright, stay here I'll hail a taxi. Don't move, I'll be one minute. *[Exit USR]*
C: *[Turns]*

[93 Scuzzy room TV]

C: *[Takes a pill]* My name is Mountford, Dawson, Rogers... My name is John, Richard, Michael. I have a sister... I have a girlfriend... I've forgotten something...

[94 Scuzzy room close up]

C: *[Opens suitcase on table and goes through its contents]*
I have an automatic camera.
I have an alarm clock.
I do not have a telephone.
I have a guidebook.
I have a fountain pen.
I have a map of the town.
These are my personal belongings.

[95 Alpine cafe]

I have 200 euros in currency, 100 euros in travellers' cheques.
I have been here for four weeks.
Here is my passport.
I have visited the camera store.
I have visited the cigarette kiosk.
I have visited the drug store.
These are for my work.

[96 Scuzzy room TV]
C: *[Gets necklace out of his pocket]*

I am just passing through.
   It is Tuesday.
   There is duty to pay on this.
   My name is Mountford.

[97 Hotel room lamp]

A: [As hotel receptionist] I'm sorry Mr. Mountford I thought you'd left.
   I'm sorry I thought you'd checked out this morning.
   I thought you had to be somewhere.
   Shouldn't you have already gone Mr. Mountford?
   [Takes off chair and mug]
   You see it's Tuesday. The maid is coming in to clean. I'll put this in the hotel safe. you won't come back for it, it doesn't matter. [Picks up gun case, takes it off]
   I'm very sorry but we need this room. We have another reservation. You only booked four nights and you should be somewhere else. [Takes table off]
   I gave you an alarm call Mr. Mountford.
C: [Moves to chair but A picks it up]
A: 7am. You should be somewhere else.
   You have an appointment. 8am.
C: Yes, I know.
A: You should have already checked out.
C: I'm leaving now.
A: You should have already gone. [Reaches into C's coat pocket and removes hotel key]
   I hope you had a pleasant stay. [Exit USL]

[98 Forest]
[99 Lake]
[101 Pier]

C: [Walks towards screen and puts case down]
A: [Joins C as Claire and holds his hand]
C: I'd love to but I can't Claire, I can't. I've already stayed longer than I should have. I got distracted. It would be lovely but I have to leave. I have to leave, my flight's

	booked now. I'm sorry. I'm sorry.
A:	Just a few more days. Three more days. My project will be finished in a couple of days then we can do whatever you want.
C:	I'd love to but I can't, I've got to go.
A:	We could leave the city for a few days.
C:	That would be great but I've had an urgent call from Head Office. They need me to finish off here and get back.
A:	A filing cabinet crisis?
C:	Yeah, I'm the only man who can sort it out, sorry.
A:	This has just been a holiday romance for you then?
C:	No! How can you say that? I haven't been here on holiday, I've been working, haven't you noticed?
A:	John, it's not funny!
C:	I know. I didn't mean that, it's been much more than that but I have to go.
A:	Is there something you're not telling me?
C:	No!
A:	Is there someone at home?
C:	No, there's no-one at home, it's not that, it's just I never thought I'd find myself here.
A:	What do you mean?
C:	In this situation.
A:	Right.
C:	With you.
A:	No, neither did I.
C:	I've got something for you, I brought you this. *[Pulls necklace out of his pocket and his passport falls out. They grab for it]*
A:	Let's have a look!
C:	No, give it me back!
A:	No, I want a look!
C:	Claire, you don't want to see...
A:	It can't be that bad. *[Opens passport]* Who are you?
C:	Give me the passport!
A:	Who do you really work for?
C:	Claire.
A:	Who sent you?

C: Claire, just give me the passport.
A: Tell me who you are!
C: Look, it's complicated.
A: I don't believe this, you stayed in my flat!
C: Claire, listen.
A: Give me my keys.
C: Listen, I'm sorry. I'm not who I said I was.
A: Give me my keys.
C: But it's different now, I've changed my mind.
A: You're here because of the Phoenix project.
C: This wasn't supposed to happen, I wasn't supposed to fall in love with you, that's why I'm going.
A: Who sent you?
C: Claire…
A: Who?
C: You know my sister.
A: What? You've seen all my work! You've been through all my things haven't you?
C: You don't have to worry!
A: I'm calling the police.
C: No, you don't have to do that, I'm leaving.
A: I was so stupid!
C: No you weren't, I'm sorry. Look, I'm going, I'm leaving, just forget about it. Give me the passport and I'll go.
A: Enjoy your trip. *[Throws passport down]*
C: *[Picks up passport and gives her the necklace]* I bought you this.
A: Wow. It's beautiful! I don't know what to say.
C: I was passing a shop, saw it in the window and thought you might like it.
A: You shouldn't have, I haven't got you anything.
C: Haven't you?
A: No.
C: Ah well, I can probably take it back.
A: Give me the necklace, now!
C: *[Putting necklace on A]* I just wanted to say thank you for showing me round and for making what would have been a really boring stay into a fun packed one. I really appreciate it.

[102 Moonlight, moon out of focus]

C: Will you come and say goodbye, tomorrow?
A: I can't.
C: Early, eight o'clock, we could make it in the park. Yeah, our bench, and we can say good-bye properly. Yeah, eight o'clock.

[103 Moonlight, moon in focus]
[104 Rooftop]

C: I'm on time. I've done what you wanted. *[Looks SL]* It's finished. I want it wrapped up. *[Looks right and up]*

[105 Looking down on Craig]

C: Hello? Are you there?

[106 Looking up at roof]

C: I want to go home.
   I'm tired.

[107 Wall door pipe]

C: I have what you want.
   I have the papers.
   Do you want to see? *[Opens case above his head, papers and packing falls out at his feet. He grabs the papers]*
   Look... Here! *[Retreats upstage]*

[108 Scuzzy room corner]

C: *[Checks his watch, moves DS and packs the case]*
A: Is she expecting you Michael?
C: No.
A: Do you have an appointment?
C: Yes.
A: What is your name?

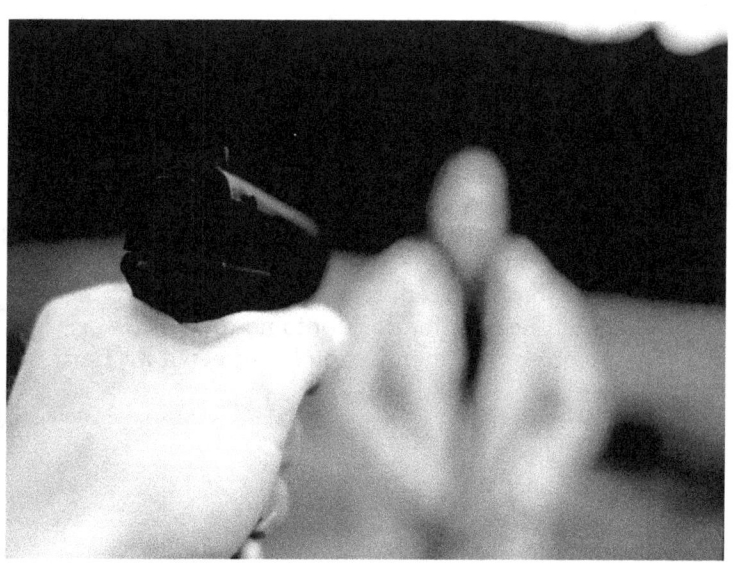

C: John.
A: What's your job?
C: I'm a salesman.
A: How long do we have here?
C: My flight leaves at twelve o'clock.
A: Have you visited the doctor?
C: Yes, I have health insurance.
A: Is she your girlfriend?
C: What do you mean?
A: Is she your girlfriend?
C: No.
A: What's wrong?
C: The nerve is exposed.
A: What are you going to do?
C: This tooth will have to be extracted.
A: I would like to meet her.
C: Come with me to the park, tomorrow.
A: I am travelling with my brother.
We're here on business.
We'll pay for this together.
C: What's the weather forecast for tomorrow?
A: There's going be a thunderstorm and then it will be sunny.
C: Will I see you there?
A: Oh yes, I'll be there.
C: *[Turns around]*

[109 Scuzzy room TV]
[110 Scuzzy room door]

C: *[Turns slowly]*

[111 Park]
[112 Claire approach 1]
[113 Claire approach 2]
[114 Claire standing]

C: *[Turns away, takes gun out of pocket and looks down at it]*

[115 Down at gun]

C: *[Looks back to where Claire would be standing]*

[116 Claire close up]
[117 Claire hand]

C: *[Points gun at Claire]*

[118 Gun and Claire out of focus]
[119 Gun and Claire in focus]

C: *[Shoots Claire]*

[120 Claire blurred close up]
[121 Falling eye 1]
[122 Falling eye 2]
[123 Falling eye 3]

C: *[Looks away lowering the gun]*

[124 Bloody face]
[125 Dead Claire]

C: *[Looks back]*

[126 Wasteland]

C: *[Wipes the gun and puts it in the case]*

[127 Plane 1]
[128 Plane 2]

C: *[Looks round to watch himself approaching on the screen]*

[129 Craig approaching door 1]
[130 Craig approaching door 2]
[131 Craig approaching door 3]
[132 Craig approaching door 4]

[133 Craig in doorway]

C: [Looks out to audience]

[134 Craig turning round]

C: [Looks back to screen]

[135 Craig walking away]

C: [Picks up case and moves towards screen]

[136 Roof outside]

C: [Turns to face audience]

[137 Roof wall, door and pipe]

C: Hello. Hello. I'm here. I have a delivery.
 Can you hear me?
 I made it. I'm on time.
 I've done what you wanted.
 It's finished.
 I want it wrapped up.
 Susan...
A: What have you done Michael?
C: I did what you wanted. There was a thunderstorm, I...
A: You've done a bad thing Michael, Claire was innocent.
C: No, she was the chemist.
A: She was innocent Michael.
C: No, they said, they said the nerve was exposed, they said it wasn't a car crash, I did it for you, I didn't want to.
A: Who are they Michael, who are they?
C: You said. I promised to come and look for you. I did it for you.
 I wanted you to be proud of me.
 I want to go home.
A: No one lives at home Michael, you're on your own.

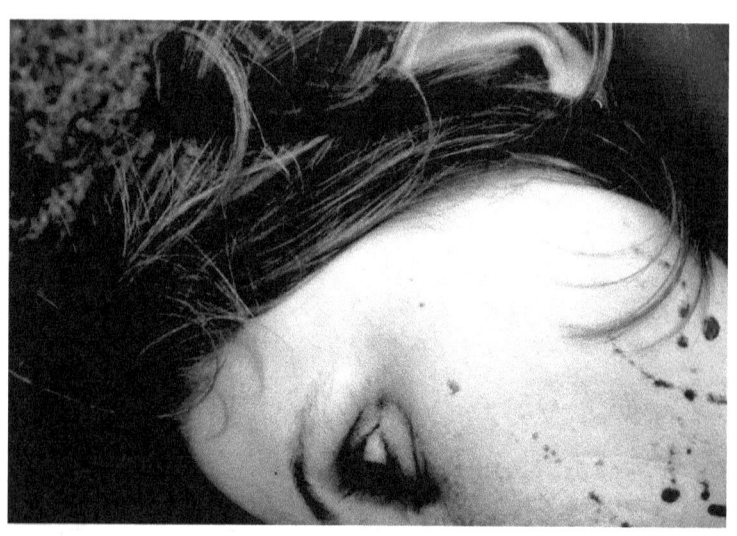

[138 Memory room]

C: You're my sister. Ich bin auf dich stoltz.
A: Haben Sie etwas zu verzollen.
C: No, no. I did what I was told.

[139 Bloody Claire face]

A: *[Indicating the suitcase]* There is duty to pay on this Herr Rogers.
C: I didn't understand the sign.
A: Please open this bag.
C: What are you looking for?
A: Your passport has expired.
C: There has been an accident. It's my girlfriend.
A: A police car is on the way.

[140 Bloody Claire hand]

C: There is someone injured.
A: Do you feel unwell Herr Rogers?
C: I can't turn off the tap.

[141 Airport Corridor]

A: Open your mouth.
C: I can't open the window.
A: This isn't my responsibility.
C: There's too much noise.
A: There is nothing I can do. *[Off to get chair]*
C: I want to go home, I want to sit down, I want a glass of water.
A: *[Returning]* Sit down Mr. Rogers, Mr. Nowicki is expecting you.
C: I'll miss my flight.
A: Are you going to be well enough to fly Mr. Mountford?

[142 Roof outside]

C: I'll miss my flight.
A: Sit down Michael. You're too late. The gate is closing.
C: I have a seat by the window.
A: It's over Michael. You were wrong. You did a bad thing.
C: Please don't go.
A: You won't see me again.

[143 A leave 1]
[144 A leave 2]
[145 A leave 3]
[146 A looks up]
[147 A leaving]
[148 A leaves]
[149 Airport corridor]
[150 Window]

C: It's Tuesday.
   I'm on holiday.
   I am a little dizzy.
   I'm taking medication.
   It's raining.

[151 Sky]

C: I'm thirty two.
   Thirty three.
   Thirty four... years old.

[152 Runway lights 1]
[153 Runway lights 2]
[154 Runway lights 3]
[155 Runway lights 4]
[156 Sky and plane]

A: *[Takes photos of the plane]*

[157 Big plane overhead]
[158 Plane moving away]
[159 Plane in distance]
A: *[The camera automatically rewinds and A puts it back in C's suitcase]*
C: *[Drops mug]*

[The slide projectors are switched off]

A: *[Takes necklace from coat pocket and exits]*

Original Programme Notes

Devised by:
Amanda Hadingue, Craig Stephens, James Yarker

Performed by: Amanda Hadingue or Heather Burton
and Craig Stephens

Slides by: Ed Dimsdale and Stan's Cafe

Music by: Nina West

Lights by: Paul Arvidson

Advisory Producer: Nick Sweeting

Administrator: Maya Kristina Paul

Thanks to: Sarah Archdeacon and Kate Chapman

An early version of this show was performed at MAC in September 2003

Be Proud Of Me was commissioned by Mousonturm, Frankfurt

Stan's Cafe is funded Arts Council England

Be Proud Of Me isn't the result of a master plan, it is the consequence of three people worrying away at a handful of ideas in a rehearsal room, knee deep in phrase books and photographic slides, for weeks on end.

We started knowing we wanted to make a show using slide projections and phrasebooks; unfortunately we didn't know what that show was. The answer has come painstakingly as we have worked with these tools and learnt the rules of the peculiar theatre world they seemed to want to make together.

Working with the slides led to a world of fragmented memory, time slippage and false perspectives. The phrase books prompted locations and encounters. They shaped our language and challenged us to use simple words to say complicated things. Whilst there has always been a story attendant to the show, it has changed many times to accommodate the show's requirements.

All this is an elaborate way of saying maybe in Be Proud Of Me the story is less important than it's telling. Maybe memory is less significant than the act of remembering.

About the illustration and design

The illustrations for the covers of these books were undertaken by students at Birmingham City University as the final module of their first-year illustration course during the Spring/Summer of 2018. The images were developed using workshops using variations of the theatre-devising methods produced by Stan's Cafe but adapted and applied to the making of visual work. The resulting work was shown in the pop-up exhibition *The Something Of Somebody Something* at AE Harris in May 2018.

The design concept of the books was produced by final year Graphic Design student Aimee Chapman. These were then further developed for print in a collaborative process between Stan's Cafe and the University's Innovation Product Support Service (IPSS) and involved helping the company with selecting appropriate DTP software, undertaking training and selecting a suitable print on demand service.

Gareth Courage
Lecturer in Illustration
Birmingham City University

www.ingramcontent.com/pod-product-compliance
Lightning Source LLC
Chambersburg PA
CBHW070104120526
44588CB00034B/2247